Amanda Gibbs, 2015

ISBN 978-0-9940750-0-0

www.amandagibbs.com

Making It

Amanda Gibbs

To the person(s) that inspired this book:
Thanks for not loving me. Unrequited love
makes writing so much more interesting. - AG

"Hi"

She blinked three times without turning to face him. She didn't need to look to know he would be just another Polo wearing, cargo short donning drunk guy at Gracie's. Apparently very drunk if the smell of Fireball and shitty beer was any indicator.

She caught the bartender Ryan's eye; he rolled his eyes, as he did roughly every hour some guy tried to engage her in pleasant conversation with the sole purpose of taking her home, maybe asking for racy pictures, definitely forgetting her name by next month.

He continued to stand there, blatantly interrupting her and her girlfriends' conversation, and judging by the cocky grin

4

she could see in her peripheral, was not
sorry about it at all.

She licked her lips, plastered the
bitchiest smile she could muster on her
burgundy painted mouth, and slowly, slowly
swiveled her barstool to face him head on.

"Can I help you, sweetie?"

Tactic number one. Speak to them as if
they are eight year old boys incapable of
tying their own shoelaces. This immediately
gave her the power in the situation and
emasculated him enough to sulk back to his
friends, licking his wounds.

He turned his head to look behind each
shoulder as if she was talking to someone
else. He cocked his eyebrow and nodded his

head, learning faster than most how this routine usually went. Usually.

"Well,"

He plopped his beer down on the wet table top and sat down, uninvited, in the empty seat next to her. Her two friends had grown tired of the drama weekends ago, and didn't even bother to pretend to pay attention.

"I don't see any 'sweeties' to assist, but if you'd like some help in the 'why am I such a rude bitch' category, I've been told I'm a good listener."

It was his turn to play the condescending card. What she didn't know was that he thrived on a challenge, and he knew she'd be one the moment she walked in wearing her cowboy boots and UFC T-shirt. What he didn't know though, was that she owned stilettos sharper than his wit, and he'd have to step up his game about 27 points before she would take *his* number. 29 if he wanted a text anytime soon.

She didn't need a second to reply, but took two just to look deep into his eyes. She concluded he was about as deep as the kiddie pools at public parks. She told him this.

"I'm sensing you're about as emotionally deep as a kiddie pool at a public park, so I won't make this conversation overly intellectually stimulating, but you know, you are just so right. My bitchiness is something I've been struggling to diagnose for years, and little did I know all it took was some Harlequin cover model with a

rejection complex to tell me. Thank you,
really, how will I ever repay you?"

"Dance with me."

She snorted.

"I'm serious"

"-ly delusional, maybe"

    He took out his wallet and pulled out a
twenty, presumably for more shots he didn't
need.

"One dance, and if you're still vehemently
repulsed by my presence at the end, I'll
give you this twenty, and I'll leave the
bar."

He was crazy. She honestly thought he was crazy at this point, but that didn't stop her interest from peaking slightly.

"So you would like me to whore off a dance to you for a measly twenty bucks?"

"Exactly."

Her friends were talking about their husbands, and accounting programs. There was nothing she hated more than accounting and marriage. She pounded back her shot of tequila, no lemon, no salt.

"Alright asshole, let's do it."

"I like you."

"Shut up and don't step on my feet."

Dustin Lynch's "Cowboys and Angels"
came on, and bowing like an 18th century
Jane Austen character, almost throwing out
his back, he invited her to the dance floor.

If she was doing this, she may as well
have fun with it. She curtsied, about as
well as a 200 pound trucker, and placed her
hands around his neck. His skin was warm,
and freckled; the summertime tan fading
away.

He placed his hands on her back, so far
up that she laughed at his politeness. She
secretly appreciated it, but she still
laughed at it. She let go of his neck with
one hand, grabbed his hand behind her, and
placed it three inches lower, where the "v"
on her lower back began.

"Do you still-"

"OWW"

It took him all of fifteen seconds to step on her toe.

"Do I still hate you?"

"Maybe answer that after I get you an icepack for your feet?"

The chorus came on, and they had to lean towards each other's ears to hear over the music. They never stopped dancing through the four "stepping-on-toe" incidents that would occur throughout the song. "Dancing" being a loose definition of the word. They would sway a few times back and forth, lose rhythm completely, and end up in hysterics over their combined dancing score of 0.2.

She wasn't sure at what point she started loosening up. Maybe it was at the bridge of the song, maybe it was when she discovered he wasn't wearing Polo; Light Blue, she thought.

He wasn't sure when he stopped feeling the need to be sarcastic. Maybe it was when she wasn't afraid to be a horribly unsexy dancer (in the sexiest way possible). Maybe it was the shots, maybe a bit of both.

"I do."

"What?"

"Still hate you."

"Oh, you do now, do you? And why is that?"

She gave him a blatant once over, ending her eye line on her own scuffed shoes in front of him.

"Where do I start?"

"I can only trace my genealogy back four generations but I'll do my best."

She laughed, and a little piggy snort made an appearance. She immediately covered her mouth in shock and turned red as Dolly Parton's lipstick.

"That was adorable."

He meant it.

"Shut up!!"

She gave up trying to hide it, and let the giggles flow. They didn't even notice the music ended until they were the only ones on the dance floor.

With the shroud of the music and other couples gone, they became acutely aware the little moment they shared was over. She let go of his neck like it was on fire, and he released his hands from behind her back with slightly more hesitation.

They stood there.

"Should we...?"

"Yeah, we should probably..."

They did an awkward shuffle back to the main area of the bar, unsure of when to say their inevitable goodbye's.

"Wait,"

He lightly grabbed her arm. She didn't swat him away.

"Here's your twenty bucks,"

He tried to pass the folded bill into her hands.

"A deals a deal."

She looked at the money, she looked at him. She wasn't sure what she was doing, but she was sure she would regret it in the morning.

"Buy me a beer and we'll call it even."

His eyes lit up like she shone her tractor headlights right at him, and he walked a respectful distance behind her up to the bar. His smile never left his face.

"What are you smiling about?"

She didn't need to look behind her to know that he was, because she was smiling too.

"I'll just get a PBR, please."

She looked at him like he just told her he was a member of the NRA.

"Is that a joke?"

"PBR, my friend, is never a joke."

She took her Guinness, he took his can
of horse pee, and they cheers'd. Well, she
cheers'd, and he over-enthusiastically tried
to smash their two glasses into a million
pieces, spilling all over her new shirt.

"Well."

She stood there, eyes to the man
upstairs, and just let the beer sink in for
a moment before she regained enough
composure to speak.

He, in the meantime, stood mouth agape,
half broken glass in one hand, not sure if
he should laugh uncontrollably, or make sure
if her shirt was alright. At the moment, he
managed to do a little of the latter, mostly
the former.

"I may need that twenty bucks after all."

She started to laugh at the ridiculousness of him, the situation, the whole night. Once she opened the door to laughing, he couldn't help himself and they were right back to the hysterics they had found themselves in ten minutes ago.

"Can I at least pay for dry cleaning?"

"It's a t-shirt."

"Okay, yes, that may be true, but on the other hand I'm not sure how else to get your number, so please just roll with it."

She looked for a pen. He already had one.

"Do you have a-"

He passed her a napkin. She scoffed. She smiled. She wrote down *her* number.

It took him seven minutes longer than she thought it would for him to text her, asking her on a date.

- *The Last Time She Went to Gracie's Solo*

Art Of Sexting

Sext #1: I love you and I mean it.

Sext #2: Tell me what your dreams are while I stroke the sensitive part of your inner thigh; where the hem of your pleated skirt barely reaches.

Sext #3: Do you want me to brush your hair?

Sext #4: I had this dream where you slowly unzipped your insecurities and bore your naked soul to me.

Sext #5: I had this dream where you held my hand. And that's it.

Sext #6: I want to make you turkey dinner and care for your well being on this planet

while at the same time wanting to rip off
your shirt and *let you make me feel things.*

Sext #7: You're perfectly imperfect.

Sext #8: *Bite me.*

Sext #9: Meet my mother.

Sext #10: Gain 300 pounds. Doesn't change a
damn thing.

Sext #11: My pillow smells like that
perfume you wore to Centre Island; you know
the one.. maybe I'm wrong, maybe it just
smells like *you.*

Sext #12: I made space for you to have a
drawer. And a spot in the toothbrush
holder. Let's go watch football.

They were at the grocery store.

They were supposed to go to dinner and a movie, standard third date procedure.

She forgot to pick up dog food after work.

They agreed to get it together.

It was in the milk aisle; they could see the reflection of their hands dangling dangerously close to each other's in the refrigerator door.

They pretended to be deeply engaged in conversation about the benefits of skim milk.

Their pinkies touched first.

She pulled away.

She relaxed.

She grabbed his hand.

He squeezed hers back.

- Buying 2% milk, and other risky decisions

"When's she happy, the whole world smiles, I swear. It's all dancing barefoot around the kitchen; all finding places to kiss that I never knew existed; laughing like the secrets of the world were hers for the taking."

- Five pints of honesty.

"I'm bisexual."

It was borderline angry, fully defensive. She was at the point in the relationship where he seemed so perfect (for her) that she started dreaming up the faults he clearly must have. Because no boy exists that knows how to both write a poem, and stand up to her father, without having a balancing fault. Like being a murderer. Kicking puppies. Saying "That's hot, threesome?" when she revealed her orientation.

She had come to the conclusion that he would be exactly like every other presentably appearing man that turned into a puddle of adolescent hormones at the thought of two girls kissing (never married, never over forty, always to please him), because that was the fault no boy had previously avoided. She played out the scene in her head a thousand different ways, each time feeling slightly more comforted by the knowledge of the predictable. He would go googly eyed, she would get upset he would respond so immaturely, but all the while be secretly relieved she wasn't dating a flawless being she couldn't compare to. Her original idea led to thoughts, thoughts to assumptions, assumptions to suspicions, and suspicion to an increasing anger that came to a head when he made her a playlist called "Just Because". Was there anything more perfect than a playlist entitled "Just Because?"

"Im bi."

"Oh, okay,"

He looked up from his phone to smile at her for a moment.

"Thanks for letting me know. Also, what do you want for dinner? I was thinking pizza, the one with the weird cheese I can't pronounce that your mom really likes and...."

She didn't remember a single thing he said after that. She only remembered the buzz of the air conditioner in the corner, the number of fake roses in her dollar store vase; the things, like them, that after that night didn't change one bit.

-Ordering bocconcini cheese pizza

What she said: Should we-?

What she thought: This was a lot easier when you threw me on the bed and there was no time to think, and this is really awkward but maybe it's only awkward because I'm making it awkward, are you feeling awkward? You're just standing there. Why are you just standing there? Why am I just standing there? Should I make the first move? I will make the first move. *Makes the first move* That was a shitty first move.

What he said: I mean, yeah, why not..

What he thought: I shouldn't have said that. That was a dick move. Of course we should. Should we? This is going to change things. Don't be stupid, it won't change things. Sex changes things. Sleeping doesn't change things. But it wasn't just sleeping, was it? I don't know, maybe I'm over thinking.

I'm definitely over thinking. Wow. She looks really cute with no makeup on.

Nervous laughter ensued. She didn't understand why she was less nervous in lingerie and a thong than she was covered head to toe. He didn't understand why his heart was beating faster looking at her covered head to toe than it ever had in the prior.

What she said: It's not like we've never done this before.

What she thought: He's never heard me snore before. He's never seen my hair in the morning. He's only seen the cultivated image of exactly what I want him to see. Two hours of prep goes into "sexy bedroom hair". Two hours. That requires nothing of actually being in bed to get it.

What he said: Just with less ugly pajamas.

They looked down at the reindeer onesies gifted to them by Aunt Selma. Not exactly the epitome of sexy, definitely the epitome of comfort. This was the first time they would sleep together. Not sex, that had happened several times. This was the first time they would lie in the same bed, fall unconscious, probably snore, definitely drool, and wake up the next morning with nowhere to go but the bathroom to brush the morning breath off their teeth. This was the first time they would sleep together in the true sense of the word.

They got into bed. They lied on their backs. They stared up at the ceiling. They were spaced a foot apart, no body part touching, not saying anything for three minutes and twelve seconds. He coughed.

She asked if he was okay. She wasn't really asking, she just wanted to put noise into the space. He looked at her. He said he was fine. He asked if she was okay...

What he said: Are you okay?
What he meant: Am I doing something wrong?

What she said: Why am I so nervous?
What she meant: Why am I so nervous?

What he said: I don't know. I am too.

Her: When do we close our eyes and stop talking?

Him: Are we supposed to spoon?

Her: Maybe just regular cuddles.

Him: Back to back?

They laughed; the nervousness melted away like the wax on the pine scented candle beside the bed. She never was one for vanilla.

They fell asleep with her head on his chest, neither one remembering falling asleep, neither one caring about the sweaty hair on the back of her neck when they woke. She dreamt of a pine forest and white dresses, him of nothing. It was the first time he hadn't had a nightmare in a month.

She was so caught up in the smell of his cotton t-shirt and baby powder deodorant that she forgot to wonder if her eyelashes looked bad with no mascara. He was so caught up in the feel of her hair brushing against his arm that he forgot to worry about snoring.

They woke up, yawned, and went to brush the morning breath off their teeth.

The End.

-sleeping together

"How am I supposed to know when to say I love you?"

She passed him the tomato plant to put on the apartment balcony. It was the first thing they had ever owned together.

"When to say I love you, or when you know you love someone?"

He reached over to rub the dirt smear off her cheek. He licked his finger first to make sure he got it all. She didn't think twice of it.

"Both."

She stopped planting for a moment to look out at the industrial view facing her. Hotels, factories, more apartments. A couple was having sex against the window across the street. She didn't look away as she said it.

"I think you know you love someone when you do things for them when it's inconvenient for you. I think you say I love you when they do too."

-*A week before the tomato plant died*

The first time he said it, they were
assembling an ikea baby crib for his
sister's newborn. He was kneeling on the
ground reading her instructions while she
lay partway under the crib, screwdriver in
hand to do the hard bits. She didn't even
hear him the first time. She wore his old
painting t shirt and a pair of roots
sweatpants, and he had just yelled at her a
half hour before for spending too much money
on Wendy's.

"I love you."

She reached her hand out to pat his knee
affectionately.

"No, babe, it's fine, you didn't shove me at
all."

She had the screwdriver in her mouth so she could use both hands to piece the thing together, making it difficult for him to understand much of what she said either. He did one of those nervous laughs reserved for 10th graders about to give a presentation on the reproductive organs, but, to his credit, he said it again quite factually and even toned, especially for a man who had only ever previously said "I love you" to his mother and goldfish.

"I love you."

She dropped the screwdriver. On her face.

"What did you just say?" It barely came out as a whisper.

"I love you."

The first time she said "I love you" was 13 weeks after he did. He was sleeping, she was propped up on her elbow staring at him, as she had been for the past three hours trying to garner the confidence to spit out the three words. It was his snore that did it. He did this thing where he simultaneously exhaled and inhaled, while making a spitting noise which included an elephantine snore. She started giggling uncontrollably, and didn't even realize at first when the words popped out.

"I love you."

It didn't matter that it would be six more months before she said it to his face, because she said it. It was out there in the universe. And she meant it.

- How she chipped her front tooth from a screwdriver

Her: If you could delete one thing off this Earth, what would it be?

Him: Kim Jong-Un...you?

Her: Tinder.

- *mid back rub conversations*

"Did you just-?"

He did a quick sniff, confirming his suspicions, and proceeded to look at her in mock horror. She was about as red as a ladybug, and completely frozen in shock.

"Oh my god. Ohmygod I am so sorry. Ohmygod."

She was absolutely mortified. He paused the TV just in time to burst into hysterics; this man had never laughed so hard in his life. Hands were grasping bellies, there was wheezing involved, all the while she had no idea what to do and continued to sit there with a pillow hiding her face while the smell set in. It was not a nice smell. Rather egg-y, in fact.

"Did you just fart in-front of me?!"

- *The night he asked her to marry him*

"Sometimes I think I'd like to start again. Sometimes I think I'd like to go back in time and never meet you at Gracie's, never get your shitty PBR spilled on me, never let you pay for my dry cleaning. Sometimes I think I'd like to have blocked your number after the 13th date proposition, not kissed you after the 14th successful one, and not said "yes" after you asked me on the Leafs Jumbotron on the 91st. Sometimes I wonder what I'd be like if I didn't have you to eat my pickles on my Big Mac, reach the Cinnamon Toast Crunch in the top cupboard, scratch the spot on my lower left back I can never reach. If I had just let time wash away your memory like the beer stain on my favourite shirt, would I be happier in the end? Was there a "happier" than what I was now? ...But then I open my eyes, see you playing NHL '15 for the third hour in a row, the dogs, the hideous vase I spent 2 hours picking out on our first trip to Home Outfitters, and I never let it get further than a passing thought. Kind of like that boyfriend I had in sixth grade; I had him, I realized pretty quickly how bad he was at kissing, and I never thought about him again."

- *The pros and cons of PBR, and other private thoughts*

"I always get so sad when I see 80 year old couples eating at restaurants, not saying anything the whole time."

She turned the pepper grinder over his soup exactly three and a half times; he didn't need to ask.

"Why?"

He poured her wine to the half way mark; she didn't need to ask.

"Because. They've been around each other so long, they have nothing left to say. I never want to be like that."

He toyed with the stem of his glass for a moment.

"But what if they're so comfortable around each other, they know each other so well, they don't always need words to communicate? They've gotten to the point where silence is comfortable...then I'd want to be exactly like that."

They ate the rest of the meal in comfortable silence.

- *Tomato Soup and Chardonnay*

"I'm walking myself down the aisle."

"Okay."

She waited. He continued eating Cinnamon Toast Crunch as if he hadn't been interrupted.

"Don't you want to know why?"

He spoke mid crunch.

"I figure-"

He chewed. Swallowed. Rubbed the milk off the corner of his mouth.

"-you're going to tell me anyways."

She flicked his ear as she walked past.

"I don't need anyone to give me away. And I'm not being given away anyways. I'm just adding to my roster of people that I love. Why do I need someone to escort me on that?"

"You don't."

"Maybe I'll get our dog to walk down the aisle with me."

"...We don't have a dog."

She patted the top of his head.

"You should probably get on that."

-Two weeks before they rescued Otis from the pound.

I promise to touch you. To tickle you. To tease you. Not too hard; never too hard; sometimes just hard enough.

I promise to challenge you. To congratulate you. To criticize you. Never meanly; always because I care; sometimes because you need it.

I promise to learn. How you like your eggs in the morning. Your sister's boyfriends' names. How to be a good husband. I'll learn because you're my teacher... I would let you lead me anywhere.

I promise to see you. To hear you. To listen. Not just when you say things; especially when you don't say things. I promise to see the things you're not ready to say, hear the things you're not ready to show, and listen to everything in-between.

I promise to laugh. To lust. To *last*.
We'll last. I know because you make me
laugh. More than anyone. I know because
you make me lust. More deeply every day;
it's insatiable. I know we'll last because
more than anything, I know <u>you</u>.

-Wedding Vows

"Babe?"

Sitting at the kitchen table, she stirred her coffee with more aggression than the sugar meekly suggested. He didn't notice, he was too busy reading the sports section of the same paper he read every day; the same time as every day; as little talking between the two of them as every day. Monotony would kill them faster than a passionate argument ever would. At least they'd have something worth fighting about.

"If you ever want to leave me,"

This got his attention, the newspaper ceased to ruffle.

"Do it here. Take my coffee, tell me it's cold, and drink a sip. If you do that, I'll know; I'll let you, no questions asked.

I'll tell you in a calm voice that it's okay, because it's a choice, being here is a choice, and I won't ever take away your right to choose. You have to choose me as fiercely as I need to choose you, and there's been nothing fierce for a long time. I love you, but I need to be loved by you, so when that day comes you take this coffee, you tell me it's cold, and you take a goddamn sip."

- The day before he cancelled the newspaper subscription

"I'm pregnant."

They were sitting, as they had been for the past three hours, working on a 2000 piece puzzle of the Amazon jungle. He was just about to place the second corner piece down, and she figured now was as an appropriate time as any. More so than the last three hours, apparently.

He dropped the puzzle piece.

She looked down at her hands, hunching her shoulders in a way that made her look more shy teenage girl, less mother to be.

He waited for the punchline. After half a minute, it never came.

"I'm going to be a dad?"

She looked up to meet his eyes once she heard no trace of anger. She had never seen him look like he was about to cry before.

"Yeah... I guess you are."

He stood up, walked over, and kissed the top of her head.

He grabbed a brush and passed it through her hair, over and over, for the next hour. Her favourite.

"Thank you."

- *Unfinished puzzles*

Buh-boom. Buh-boom. Buh-boom.

Breathe.

"Hi."

Groan.

"What time is it?"

Giggle.

"Early."

Stretch.

"Breakfast?"

Sheets ruffling.

"Eggs?"

Halt.

"I love you."

Feet thudding.

"Sunny side up it is."

More feet thudding.

"Wh- ?"

Against a wall.

"You're crazy."

Kissing.

"Eggs!"

Sigh. Shower running. Pan frying. Sizzle.

"That smells fantastic."

"You're fantastic."

Newspaper flipping.

"Work?"

Another sigh.

"No, not today."

Raised eyebrow.

"Why?"

"You, that's why."

*Blush. Hitched breath. Fingers run
nervously through freshly washed hair.
Lavender. Silence. More silence. Cleared
throats. Eyes to the table. Eyes to eyes.*

"We're...?"

"We're going to. We're going to make it."

*Laughter. Hands reaching. Hands finding.
Souls touching.*

Trust.

Respect.

Humour.

The End.

- Morning of the 30th Anniversary

She was sitting on the couch eating a
bowl of spicy Doritos, resting her tired
feet across his lap. Him, reading glasses
perched on the bridge of his slightly
crooked nose, cheesy romance novel in hand.
There were only so many metaphysics books
one could read before a needed Harlequin
break. He was deeply engrossed in the
plight of the emotionally damaged cowboy
when she interrupted him mid-Dorito.

"Do you-"

(she paused to transfer cheese sauce from
the corner of her mouth to her pants)

"think there's such a thing as soul-mates?"

He took a few moments to answer. She
thought he was being pensive, he was just
finishing the chapter. He dog eared the

58

$2.99 corner store special, and started massaging her feet while he thought about her question. She was nothing if not surprising. He slid his thumb over her arch.

"I don't think there's one soulmate for one thing. I think we have soul-mates for each different thing, whether it's a music soulmate, food soulmate, someone who happens to be your soulmate in loving the exact same scene in the same episode of Lost."

He grazed the ball of her foot just the way she liked.

"Okay... well then how do you know which one to choose?"

She pretended to fiddle with the TV remote to look as uninterested and casual about the answer as possible. Really, she was feeling about as casual as the cathedral marriage between the cowboy and damsel in distress.

"Well, for me, I chose my soulmate in the big stuff. Views on human rights, religious beliefs, whether or not we should buy pulp free orange juice; the things that would make "us" pretty impossible to survive if we didn't agree on."

He wrapped a blanket around her feet and tucked them in, they were ice cold as usual.

"I think I just decided I married the right guy"

"I'm still undecided"

"Says the one who wouldn't have his chick lit fix if it wasn't for me"

She flicked the TV on and they watched four
episodes of Sons Of Anarchy without bringing
it up again. They went to bed, smiling, and
she wasn't going to say anything until he
whispered in her ear, giving her butt a
little smack as he did,

"It is pretty nice that I don't have to
fight with you about crunchy peanut butter
though."

-soulmates

Her: How do we know it's over?

Him: When you feel comfortable peeing in
front of me.

Her: You're an ass. I'm serious.

Him: ...Maybe it's over when I stop being
the person you think about at 2pm, when you
have a million other things you should be
thinking about, and I start being the memory
at 2am when there's nothing else left.

www.ingramcontent.com/pod-product-compliance
Lightning Source LLC
Chambersburg PA
CBHW020512100426
42813CB00030B/3208/J